AMICUS LEARNING

CUPCAKE-OPEDIA

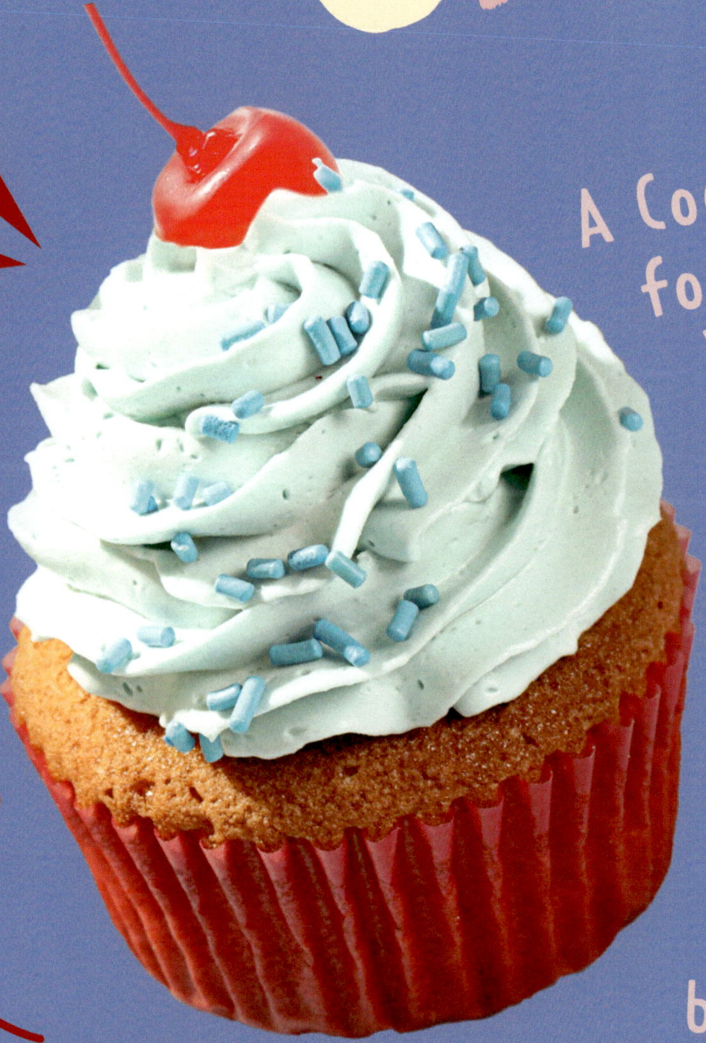

A Cookbook for Kids Who Love CUPCAKES

by Teresa Klepinger

AMICUS HIGH INTEREST is published by
Amicus Learning, an imprint of Amicus
P.O. Box 227, Mankato, MN 56002
www.amicuspublishing.us

LIBRARY OF CONGRESS CATALOGING-IN-PUBLICATION DATA
Names: Klepinger, Teresa author
Title: Cupcake-opedia : a cookbook for kids who love cupcakes / by Teresa Klepinger.
Other titles: Cupcakeopedia
Description: Mankato, Minnesota : Amicus Learning, [2026] | Series: Kids in the kitchen | Audience: Ages
   7–10 | Audience: Grades 4–6 | Summary: "Simple homemade cupcake recipes for tweens and teens
   inspire kids to experiment in the kitchen. This delightful guide features easy-to-follow recipes,
   decorating ideas, safety tips, a glossary, and party-hosting tips. Perfect for budding chefs to unleash
   their creativity!"–Provided by publisher.
Identifiers: LCCN 2025019511 (print) | LCCN 2025019512 (ebook) | ISBN 9798892008709 library binding |
   ISBN 9798892009362 paperback | ISBN 9798896850021 ebook
Subjects: LCSH: Cupcakes–Juvenile literature | LCGFT: Cookbooks
Classification: LCC TX771 .K584 2026 (print) | LCC TX771 (ebook) | DDC LC record available at
   https://lccn.loc.gov/2025019511
LC ebook record available at https://lccn.loc.gov/2025019512

PHOTO CREDITS: Amicus/Emily Dietz, 22 (top), 24, 30 (top); Kim Pfeffer, 7; Freepik, cover, 1; Getty
Images/Juj Winn, 5, Michael Hall, 13; Shutterstock/AB-7272, 14 (bottom), Africa Studio, 11, Arancio, 8,
Arina P Habich, 12 (left), Carey Jaman, 26 (top), Cecilia Di Dio, 22 (bottom), Elena Veselova, 14 (top),
Happy Author, 21 (bottom), Natallia Yeupak, 26 (bottom), Nataly Studio, 30 (bottom), New Africa, 4,
Petroos, 21 (top), Pixel-Shot, 12 (right), riyantiajeng, 27, Robilad Co, 18 (top), Rui Elena, 17, Soho A
Studio, 18 (bottom), Tatiana Vorona, 29

EDITOR: Rebecca Glaser
SERIES DESIGNER: Kim Pfeffer
BOOK DESIGNER: Emily Dietz

Printed in the United States of America

CONTENTS

WE LOVE CUPCAKES!

Why do people love **CUPCAKES** so much? Well, they taste good, for starters. They're easy to hold, so you don't need a plate or silverware. (A napkin might be nice, though.) Maybe best of all, bakers can be so creative with them! But when was the cupcake invented? And why is it called a cupcake?

It's hard to say for sure. The first cookbook to feature a recipe for cupcakes appeared in 1796. This dessert got its name for two reasons. One, the ingredients were measured in cups instead of by weight, like most cooks did back then. Two, the cakes were baked in cups, which made them easier to manage. (Muffin tins hadn't been invented yet.) By the early 1800s, the "cup cake" had become popular.

Now cupcakes are filled, layered, and swirled. Decorations range from holiday themes to team colors and works of art fit for a wedding. As you try out these cupcake recipes, let your imagination run wild! Can you make up your own flavors? How will you decorate these inventions? Enjoy the creativity—and take pictures!

COOKING GLOSSARY

BEAT To stir rapidly with a whisk or electric mixer to add air.

BLEND To gently combine dry ingredients to make a smooth mixture.

MIX To stir until the ingredients are combined well, often combining liquids and dry ingredients.

STIR To use a spoon to loosely combine ingredients.

WHISK To stir with a tool made with loops of wire, also called a whisk. Use a fork if you don't have a whisk.

METRIC CONVERSION CHART

1 teaspoon (tsp.) = 5 ml

1 tablespoon (Tbsp.) = 15 ml

¼ cup = 60 ml

⅓ cup = 80 ml

½ cup = 120 ml

1 cup = 240 ml

1 quart = 1 liter

1 gallon = 4 liters

1 ounce (oz.) = 28 g

16 oz. = 460 g

GETTING READY

 Wash your hands.

 Wear an apron to protect your clothes.

 Tie back loose hair.

 Read the whole recipe first.

 Gather all your ingredients before you start.

 Ask for an adult's help if you're not sure how to do something.

HELPFUL TIPS

- Always use **OVEN MITTS** for taking food out of the oven.

- You'll need a **FLEXIBLE SPATULA** for many of these recipes. It's a long-handled tool with a flexible nylon or silicone end for scooping and scraping.

- **PLAN AHEAD**. Ingredients mix better at room temperature. Set out butter and eggs a few hours before you're ready to bake.

- A **PASTRY BAG** is handy for squeezing frosting into fun designs. If you don't have one, see the DIY instructions on page 12.

BASIC VANILLA CUPCAKES

This is where it all starts.
Once you learn this recipe, the possibilities are endless!

SERVINGS: 12

TIME:

- 45 minutes, plus cooling time

INGREDIENTS

- 1¼ cups flour
- 1¼ tsp. baking powder
- ½ tsp. salt
- ½ cup (1 stick) butter, room temperature
- ¾ cup sugar
- 2 eggs, room temperature
- 1 tsp. vanilla extract
- ⅓ cup milk

EQUIPMENT

- Medium bowl
- Large bowl
- Electric mixer
- Flexible spatula
- Measuring cups and spoons
- Muffin tin, regular size
- Paper baking cups
- Toothpicks

STEPS

1. **PREP.** Preheat oven to 350°F (180°C). Put a paper baking cup in each muffin cup.

2. **STIR.** In the medium bowl, stir together the flour, baking powder, and salt.

3. **BEAT.** In the large bowl, beat the butter with the electric mixer for 30 seconds. Add the sugar, about ¼ cup at a time and mix well, scraping the sides of the bowl with the spatula. Beat for 2 minutes more to get it light and fluffy. Add the eggs, one at a time, and beat well after each one. Beat in the vanilla extract.

4. **COMBINE.** While beating on low speed, add about ⅓ of the flour mixture, then ½ of the milk, then another ⅓ of the flour, the rest of the milk, and end with the rest of the flour. Beat just until it looks blended.

5. **POUR.** Pour the batter evenly into the muffin cups, filling them about two-thirds full. It's tricky! Use a spoon or a measuring cup.

6. **BAKE AND FROST.** Bake for 18–20 minutes. Check after 18 minutes by sticking a toothpick in the middle of one. If it comes out clean (or with just a crumb or two), they're done. They should be just a bit golden brown. Cool in the pan for 5 minutes, then put them on a wire rack. When they're completely cool, frost with vanilla frosting (See p. 10).

FROSTING & DECORATING BASICS

Every cupcake needs frosting and decorations! Start with this basic frosting recipe, then try different flavors.

SERVINGS: 12

TIME:

- 10 minutes

INGREDIENTS

- 3 cups powdered sugar
- ⅓ cup butter, room temperature
- 1 tsp. vanilla extract
- 1–2 Tbsp. milk
- Food coloring (optional)

EQUIPMENT

- Large bowl
- Electric mixer
- Flexible spatula
- Knife
- Pastry bag and tips (optional)

STEPS

1. **BLEND.** In the large bowl, blend butter and powdered sugar with the electric mixer on low speed. Use short bursts, so the sugar doesn't fly everywhere.

2. **ADD.** Add vanilla and 1 Tbsp. of milk. If you want a different color, add food coloring in this step.

3. **BLEND AGAIN.** Blend until the frosting is smooth and spreadable. Add a small amount of milk if it's too dry.

GETTING STARTED WITH FROSTING

Start by scooping up frosting with a knife and spreading it on top of the cupcake. Try these tips to make it extra special:

- Swirl the knife back and forth to make wavy lines.

- Touch the flat side of the knife to the frosting and lift straight up to make peaks.

- Draw a pattern in the the frosting with the tip of your knife or a chopstick.

FANCY FROSTING

DIY PASTRY BAG

Snip about ½ inch (1.25 cm) off the corner of a resealable plastic bag. Push a decorating tip (found in the cake mix aisle) into the corner until it sticks about halfway out of the hole. Fold the sides of the bag down and scoop frosting into it. Twist the top closed and squeeze with steady pressure to make a stream of frosting come out.

PASTRY BAG TIPS

- The frosting should be thin enough to pass easily through the tip, or it will squeeze out around it. Think creamy, not paste-y.

- Make some extra frosting and practice on a plate with different tips.

- Start on the outside edge of the cupcake and spiral around to the center. Pull the tip up to end it.

- Use the small round tip for drawing lines and writing words.

OTHER WAYS TO DECORATE

- Sprinkles! They come in all colors and shapes, from clear crystals to sparkly dust to holiday shapes.

- Dip the top of the cupcake in sprinkles, nuts, shredded coconut, small candies, or whatever you like.

- Trim fruit snack rolls into shapes or cut shapes from jelly candies.

- Top the cupcake with a sugar figure. They come in almost any shape—eyeballs, bugs, flowers, snowflakes, soccer balls, and more! Check the decorating section of the baking aisle at the grocery store, a craft store, or online.

- Top the cupcake with shaped grahams, animal crackers, or gingerbread figures.

PINK LEMONADE CUPCAKES

Bursting with tangy citrus flavor and topped with a delicious lemon frosting, these cupcakes are perfect for a summer party.

SERVINGS: 12

TIME:

- 1 hour

EQUIPMENT

- Medium bowl
- Large bowl
- Electric mixer
- Flexible spatula
- Measuring cups and spoons
- Egg separator (or check online for how to do it without one)
- Muffin tin, regular size
- Paper baking cups
- Toothpicks

- 1¼ cups flour
- 1½ tsp. baking powder
- ¼ tsp. salt
- 3 Tbsp. butter
- ¾ cup sugar
- 3 egg whites, room temperature
- 1¼ tsp. vanilla extract
- ¼ cup milk
- ¼ cup thawed pink lemonade concentrate (from 12-oz. can)

- 3 cups powdered sugar
- ⅓ cup butter, softened
- 3–4 Tbsp. thawed pink lemonade concentrate

STEPS

1. **PREP.** Preheat oven to 350°F (180°C). Put a paper baking cup in each muffin cup.

2. **STIR.** In the medium bowl, stir together the flour, baking powder, and salt.

3. **BEAT.** In the large bowl, beat the butter with the electric mixer for 30 seconds. Add the sugar, about ¼ cup at a time and mix well, scraping the sides of the bowl with the spatula. Beat for 2 minutes more to get it light and fluffy. Add the egg whites, one at a time, and beat well after each one. Beat in the vanilla extract.

4. **COMBINE.** While beating on low speed, add about ⅓ of the flour mixture, then ½ of the milk and lemonade, then another ⅓ of the flour, the rest of the milk and lemonade, and end with the rest of the flour. Beat just until it looks blended.

5. **BAKE.** Divide the batter evenly between the muffin cups. Bake 18–20 minutes or until a toothpick poked in the middle comes out clean. Cool for 5 minutes, then put them on a wire rack to cool the rest of the way.

6. **FROST.** In the large bowl (cleaned), beat the powdered sugar and butter on low speed. Add 3 Tbsp. of lemonade and beat until spreadable. Add 1 more Tbsp. of lemonade if needed. Spread the frosting on cooled cupcakes.

RECIPE 4

CHOCOLATE MUG CAKE

What if you need your own personal cupcake NOW? Make a mug cake!

SERVINGS: 1

TIME:

- 5 minutes

EQUIPMENT

- 12-oz. microwave safe mug, or bigger (Check by pouring 12 oz. of water into it.)
- Cooking spray
- Measuring spoons
- Spoon for stirring

INGREDIENTS

- 3 Tbsp. flour
- 2 Tbsp. sugar
- 1 Tbsp. unsweetened cocoa powder
- ¼ tsp. baking powder
- Dash of salt (2 shakes of a salt shaker)
- 1 Tbsp. vegetable oil
- ⅛ tsp. vanilla extract (add more to taste)
- Optional add-ins: 1 Tbsp. chocolate chips, mini marshmallows, nuts, etc.

STEPS

1. **PREP.** Spray the inside of the mug with cooking spray.

2. **STIR.** In the mug, add the flour, sugar, cocoa powder, baking powder, and salt, and stir together.

3. **POUR.** Pour in milk, oil, and vanilla and stir until it's smooth. Scrape the bottom of the mug to get all the dry ingredients mixed in.

4. **ADD.** Add chocolate chips or your favorite extra ingredient.

5. **COOK.** Microwave it for 70 to 90 seconds on high, or until it's just a bit shiny on top. Let it sit in the microwave for 1 more minute to finish cooking on its own.

6. **ENJOY!** Top with mini marshmallows and eat your hot cocoa with a fork!

SAFETY FIRST!

For microwave cooking, pick a mug with no metal. A ceramic mug might say "microwave safe" on the bottom. If it doesn't, and you're not sure, fill it with water and cook it for a minute. If the handle doesn't get hot (use a hot pad when checking!), it's safe.

BLUEBERRY LEMON CUPCAKES

The brightness of lemon and an explosion of juice in every bite!

SERVINGS: 12

TIME:

- 1 hour 20 minutes, plus cooling time

EQUIPMENT

- Large, medium, and small bowls
- Electric mixer
- Flexible spatula
- Measuring cups and spoons
- Grater
- Muffin tin, regular size
- Paper baking cups
- Toothpicks

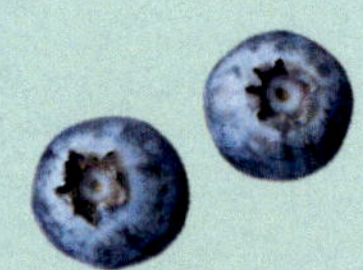

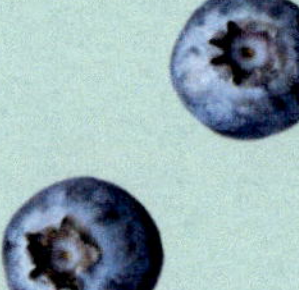

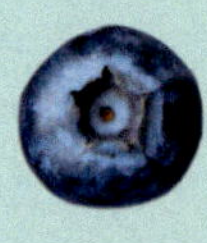

- 1¼ cups flour
- 1¼ tsp. baking powder
- ¼ tsp. salt
- ½ cup (1 stick) butter, room temperature
- ¾ cup sugar
- 2 eggs, room temperature
- 1 Tbsp. grated lemon peel (You'll need 2 lemons)
- ½ tsp. vanilla extract
- ⅓ cup milk
- 2 cups fresh blueberries, washed and dried, divided
- 1 Tbsp. flour

- All the ingredients for Basic Vanilla Frosting (See p. 10.)
- 2 tsp. grated lemon peel

STEPS

1. **PREP.** Preheat oven to 350°F (180°C). Put a paper baking cup in each muffin cup. Using the small holes on the grater, grate just the yellow part of the lemon peel. Toss 1½ cups blueberries in a small bowl with 1 Tbsp. of flour.

2. **STIR.** In the medium bowl, stir together the flour, baking powder, and salt.

3. **BEAT.** In the large bowl, beat the butter with the electric mixer for 30 seconds. Add the sugar, about ¼ cup at a time and mix it well, scraping the sides of the bowl with the spatula. Beat for 2 minutes more to get it light and fluffy. Add the eggs, one at a time, and beat well after each one. Beat in the grated lemon peel and vanilla extract.

4. **COMBINE.** On low speed, add ⅓ of the flour, then ½ of the milk, then ⅓ of the flour, the rest of the milk, and end with the rest of the flour. Beat just until it looks blended.

5. **POUR.** Pour the batter evenly into the muffin cups, filling them about half full. Sprinkle the floured blueberries evenly over each muffin cup.

6. **BAKE AND FROST.** Bake 18–20 minutes or until a toothpick poked in the middle comes out clean. While cupcakes bake, mix grated lemon peel with vanilla frosting. When cupcakes are cool, frost them with lemon frosting and decorate with blueberries.

RECIPE 6

BANANA CHOCOLATE CHIP CUPCAKES

Cupcakes for breakfast? Why not? Fruit and protein included!

SERVINGS: 12

TIME:

- 1 hour 40 minutes

CUPCAKE INGREDIENTS

- All the ingredients for Basic Vanilla Cupcakes (See p. 8.)
- 2 very ripe bananas (must have lots of dark spots), mashed, about 1 cup
- ¾ cup mini chocolate chips

FROSTING INGREDIENTS

- 1 cup creamy peanut butter
- ⅓ cup butter, room temperature
- 2 cups powdered sugar
- 3 Tbsp. milk

EQUIPMENT

- Electric mixer
- Large, medium, and small bowls
- Fork
- Flexible spatula
- Measuring cups and spoons
- Muffin tin, regular size
- Paper baking cups
- Toothpicks

STEPS

1. **MASH BANANAS.** Squish bananas in a small bowl with a fork.

2. **MAKE CUPCAKES.** Follow the Basic Vanilla Cupcakes recipe on page 8 EXCEPT: use only ⅓ cup butter, 2 Tbsp. milk, and add 1 cup of mashed banana. Stir in the chocolate chips. Fill muffin cups and bake.

3. **BEAT.** While the cupcakes bake, beat the butter and peanut butter in a clean large bowl. When it is creamy, add the powdered sugar gradually. Add 1 Tbsp. of milk if it gets too thick.

4. **BEAT MORE.** Beat the frosting on high speed for 3 minutes, scraping down the sides of the bowl. This will make it light and fluffy.

5. **FROST.** Spread or pipe the frosting onto the cupcakes. If you don't like peanut butter, chocolate frosting is great on these, too!

PEPPERMINT SWIRL CUPCAKES

One bite vanilla. One bite peppermint. One bite both! Perfect for holiday gatherings, these are sure to please your guests.

SERVINGS: 12

TIME:

- 1 hour 30 minutes

EQUIPMENT

- Electric mixer
- Rolling pin and resealable bag
- Large and medium bowl
- Flexible spatula
- Measuring cups and spoons
- Muffin tin, regular size
- Paper baking cups
- Toothpicks

- All the ingredients for Basic Vanilla Cupcakes (See p. 8.)
- ⅛ tsp. peppermint extract
- Red paste or gel food color

- 2½ cups powdered sugar
- ¼ cup butter, room temperature
- ½ tsp. peppermint extract
- 3-4 Tbsp. milk

- 6-10 peppermint candies, crushed (Place them in a resealable bag and pound them with the rolling pin.)

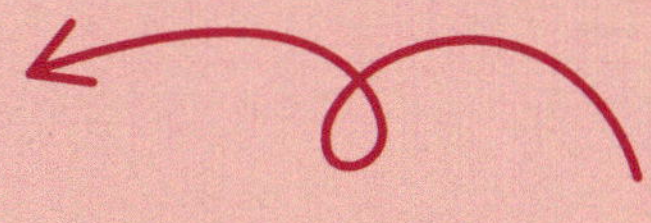

STEPS

1. **MAKE CUPCAKES.** Follow the Basic Vanilla Cupcakes recipe on page 8 EXCEPT: spoon 1 cup of the batter into a medium bowl. Stir in ⅛ tsp. peppermint extract and a few drops of red food coloring.

2. **FILL CUPS.** In each muffin cup, spoon about 1 Tbsp. of white batter, 1 Tbsp. of pink batter, and 1 Tbsp. of white batter.

3. **SWIRL.** Draw an "S" in the cake batter with a knife or chopstick to swirl colors. Swirl each cup once. Do not stir!

4. **BAKE.** Bake for 18-20 minutes, until toothpick poked in the center of a cupcake comes out clean. Cool in the pan for 5 minutes. Then put the cupcakes on a wire rack to cool the rest of the way.

5. **MAKE FROSTING.** While cupcakes cool, in a large bowl, beat the powdered sugar, butter, peppermint extract, and 2 Tbsp. of milk on low speed until it starts to mix. Then beat on medium speed until the frosting is smooth. Add more milk, 1 tsp. at a time, until it is spreadable.

6. **FROST.** Spread or pipe the frosting onto the cupcakes. Sprinkle with crushed peppermint candy.

GINGERSNAP CHEESECAKE CUPCAKES

Cozy up for fall with this yummy cupcake and a mug of apple cider!

SERVINGS: 12

TIME:

- 45 minutes (prep)
- 4 hours (refrigeration)

EQUIPMENT

- Large and medium bowl
- Electric mixer
- Food processor or rolling pin with a resealable bag
- Flexible spatula
- Measuring cups and spoons
- Muffin tin, regular size
- Paper baking cups

INGREDIENTS

- 1½ cups gingersnap cookie crumbs (Pulse them in a food processor, or pound them in a resealable bag with a rolling pin.)
- ¼ cup butter, melted
- 16 oz. full-fat cream cheese (2 blocks), room temperature
- 1 cup sugar
- 2 eggs, room temperature
- 2 Tbsp. molasses
- 1 tsp. vanilla extract
- 1 tsp. ground ginger
- ½ tsp. ground cinnamon
- ½ tsp. ground nutmeg
- ¼ tsp. ground cloves
- Whipped cream

STEPS

1. **PREP.** Preheat oven to 325°F (165°C). Put a paper baking cup in each muffin cup.

2. **MAKE CRUST.** In your medium bowl, mix the gingersnap crumbs with melted butter. Stir until the crumbs are evenly coated. Spoon 2 Tbsp. of crumbs into each muffin cup and press them down. Bake about 8 minutes or until they don't look wet. Let them cool while you make the filling.

3. **MAKE FILLING.** In the large mixing bowl, beat the cream cheese and sugar together until they're light and fluffy, about 2–3 minutes. Scrape the sides of the bowl as you go.

4. **BEAT.** Add the eggs and beat for 1 minute. Add the molasses, vanilla, and spices, and beat until it's well mixed.

5. **FILL.** Fill the muffin cups evenly with the cream cheese mixture. They should be filled almost to the top. Bake for 22–25 minutes or until the edges are firm. The center should jiggle only slightly when the muffin tin is moved.

6. **COOL.** Let cool for 1 hour. Then move them to a covered container and refrigerate them for at least 4 hours or overnight. Serve with a squirt of whipped cream and a sprinkle of cinnamon!

Don't like gingersnaps? Try these other cheesecake flavors.

CHOCOLATE CHEESECAKE

CRUST: Chocolate cookies

FILLING: Use the recipe on p. 25, but do not add molasses or spices. Add 2 Tbsp. chocolate syrup instead.

TOPPING: Whipped cream and marshmallows

FRUITY CHEESECAKE

CRUST: Graham crackers

FILLING: Use the recipe on p. 25, but do not add molasses or spices.

TOPPING: Fruity pie filling (your choice!)

PUMPKIN CHEESECAKE
CRUST: Graham crackers
FILLING: Use the recipe on pg 25, but do not add molasses or spices. Add 2 Tbsp. pumpkin puree instead.
TOPPING: Whipped cream

BOSTON CREAM CUPCAKES

The Boston Cream Pie was invented at a hotel in Boston in 1856. Now you can have it as a cupcake!

SERVINGS: 12

TIME:

- 1 hour 45 minutes

INGREDIENTS

- All the ingredients for Basic Vanilla Cupcakes (See p. 8.)
- 1 box (4-serving size) vanilla instant pudding
- 1¾ cups milk (Not fat free; it won't thicken.)

FROSTING INGREDIENTS

- ⅓ cup butter
- 2 oz. unsweetened baking chocolate
- ½ cup powdered sugar
- 1 tsp. vanilla extract
- 3 Tbsp. milk

EQUIPMENT

- Electric mixer
- Large and medium bowl
- Flexible spatula
- Wooden spoon
- Measuring cups and spoons
- Whisk
- Melon baller (for scooping out balls of cupcake)
- 1-quart saucepan
- Muffin tin, regular size
- Paper baking cups
- Toothpicks

STEPS

1. **MAKE CUPCAKES.** Follow the recipe for vanilla cupcakes on page 8.

2. **MAKE FILLING.** While the cupcakes bake, make the vanilla pudding. Follow package directions, BUT use only 1¾ cups milk.

3. **SCOOP.** After the cupcakes are cool, use the melon baller to scoop out the center of each cupcake. The hole should be about 1 inch (2.5 cm) wide and reach almost to the bottom. Yes, you can eat what you scoop out!

4. **FILL.** Use a regular spoon to fill each hole with pudding.

5. **MAKE FROSTING.** In a 1-quart saucepan, melt the butter and chocolate over very low heat. Add powdered sugar and vanilla and stir. Add the milk, 1 Tbsp. at a time, until the mixture is smooth. You might need only 2 Tbsp. Cook until it starts to bubble around the edges. Pour the frosting into another container and cool it in the refrigerator for 15 minutes or until it is just warm, not hot.

6. **FROST.** Spoon frosting onto the cupcakes and spread with a knife or the back of the spoon. Enjoy!

PRO TIP

When a recipe says to beat for a specific time, follow it! Beating adds air, blends ingredients, supports structure for rising, and activates thickeners in pudding. Skipping this step can affect texture, rise, and thickness—so mix like the instructions say!

SNOWMAN CUPCAKES

Have a snowman cupcake decorating contest with your family or friends! Use a boxed cake mix to whip these up fast.

SERVINGS: 24

TIME:

- 1 hour

EQUIPMENT

- Large bowl
- Electric mixer
- Flexible spatula
- Measuring cups and spoons
- Muffin tin, regular size
- Paper baking cups
- Toothpicks

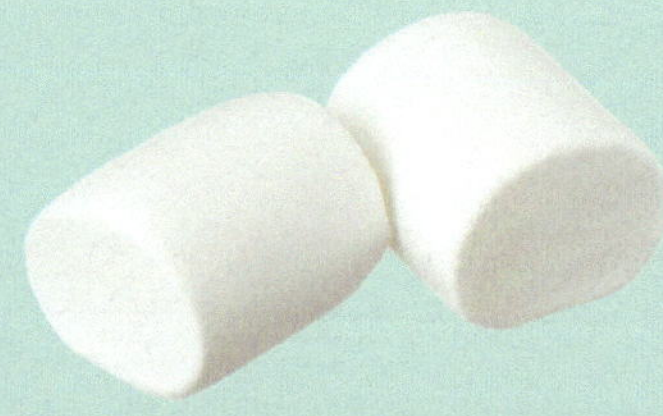

- 1 white cake mix
- Oil and eggs according to the cake mix instructions
- 1 can of white frosting (Vanilla and cream cheese are both good!)
- 1 bag of large marshmallows
- Pretzel sticks (short and thin)
- Sprinkles in different shapes, like dots, balls, and stars
- Small candies
- Fruit snack rolls
- White sugar sprinkles
- Tubes of cake decorating writing gel (color is up to you)

STEPS

1. **BAKE CUPCAKES.** Follow package instructions.

2. **FROST.** After cupcakes cool, frost the cupcakes. Sprinkle the cupcakes with white sugar crystals.

3. **CREATE HEAD.** Lay a marshmallow down to create the snowman face with cake decorating gel or sprinkles. Use a toothpick and a bit of frosting to add sprinkles for eyes, nose, or mouth. Set the marshmallow on top of the cupcake.

4. **DECORATE.** Cut a strip of fruit roll to lay across the head, frosting the ends down and placing candies over the "ears" as earmuffs. Use frosting to glue on a candy hat. Cut a strip of fruit roll and wrap around its neck as a scarf.

5. **ADD ARMS.** Stick a pretzel "arm" into the cupcake on either side of the head. If you want, cut out mittens from gummy candies or fruit roll and attach them to the ends of the pretzels.

6. **ADD BUTTONS.** Press 2 or 3 candies into the cupcake frosting as buttons. It's done! Now, do you have the heart to eat it?

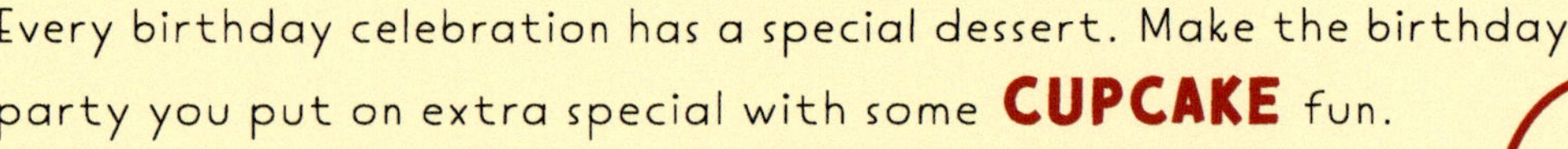

HOST A BIRTHDAY PARTY!

Every birthday celebration has a special dessert. Make the birthday party you put on extra special with some **CUPCAKE** fun.

- **GUEST LIST/FOOD ALLERGIES:** Send out your invitations. Be sure to find out if anyone has food allergies. You might need gluten free or dairy free options. You definitely need everyone to feel included in the party!

- **SET UP & PRESENTATION:** Provide undecorated cupcakes, a few bowls of different colored frosting, and several options for decorating the tops of the cupcakes. Decorate the table with balloons and set out birthday plates and napkins.

- **BE A GOOD HOST:** Welcome your guests and let them know you're glad they came. Make sure they know everyone's names.

- **HAVE FUN:** Plan a couple of games. Play upbeat music. Don't forget to sing "Happy Birthday" to the guest of honor.

- **CLEAN UP:** Have garbage bags ready for everyone to help with cleaning. That way, it's done in a snap!

Everyone loves a birthday party! With just a little planning, and delicious cupcake recipes, yours will be a blast!